Put It Down

Going from Bullied to Bold

by

Maya Claridge

Copyright © 2016 by Maya Claridge

Published by Global Publishing Group

GlobalPublishingGroupLLC@gmail.com

DISCLAIMER

This is a work of non-fiction. All rights reserved. In accordance with the U.S.Copyright Act of 1976, the scanning, uploading, and electronic sharing of any part of this book without the permission of the publisher is unlawful piracy and theft of the author's intellectual property. If you would like to use material from the book (other than for review purposes), prior written permission must be obtained by contacting GlobalPublishingGroupLLC@gmail.com

This book is purely the opinion and perspective of the author and does not necessarily represent the opinions or views of Global Publishing Group LLC. The conversations and events depicted in this book are presented in a manner to provide the reader with the general context of what was said and not intended to be a transcript.

Names have been changed to protect the innocent and more so the guilty.

Non-fiction. Printed in the United States of America.

First Edition Printed March 2016

10 9 8 7 6 5 4 3 2 1

ISBN 978-0-9968799-2-7

This book is dedicated to all of the people
who have ever been bullied
and to those who have lost family members
or friends due to bullying.

Stop Hate…Before it's too Late

www.BulliedToBold.com

INTRODUCTION

My name is Maya Claridge and I was bullied.

A few years ago I would not have been able to say or write those words because I was too ashamed to admit what was happening. I was too afraid to tell anyone.

Because...

It was my fault. That's what I believed. It was my fault that I was being bullied. I brought it on myself. I caused it. I was to blame.

You see...

IF I was prettier... IF I was skinnier... IF my teeth were straighter... IF I was smarter... IF I looked different... IF I acted different... IF I had more money... IF I had better clothes...IF I was more talented... IF I wasn't so weird...IF I wasn't annoying... IF I wasn't ME... IF I wasn't me...none of this would be happening.

If only I wasn't me.

> **When you're being bullied you start to wish you could be someone else...anyone else.**

CHAPTER ONE

FRENEMIES

I was in fifth grade when the bullying began.

A new school had opened in our community and my parents enrolled me. I knew a few kids from my previous school but most of the kids were new to me. Since this was the first year of the school, everyone was considered a "new" kid, which put us all on an even playing field, at least in the beginning.

Within the first few months of school I became friends with three girls named Riley, Erin and Chelsea. We did all of the normal fifth grade girl things together. We hung out together at recess and sat together at lunch.

We went to see movies, had sleepovers and giggled about boys we liked. We told each other secrets, painted nails and shopped at the mall and for that first half of the year we were inseparable and everything was good.

Then, slowly, things began to change.

One Saturday afternoon while we were all at the mall they decided that each of us should buy a gift for another girl in the group; something little to symbolize our friendship. We all separated to buy our gifts and when we met back up, I was shocked and devastated. Each of the girls had bought for someone but no one had bought a gift for me. I tried to tell myself that it was an accident, a mistake, that they hadn't purposefully excluded me; but deep down I think I knew otherwise. To add insult to injury, no one even apologized. They exchanged gifts right in front of me, never acknowledging that I had been forgotten.

You know that feeling you get in your stomach when someone says something that hurts you? It's like your stomach instantly hollows out and the emptiness is nauseating. That's how I felt at that moment but I was too embarrassed to say anything. I just plastered a fake smile on my face and pretended not to care.

> ➤ **Being excluded hurts.**

On Friday nights we would meet at the local Rec Center for Kids Night Out. It was fun. We would hang out, eat candy, dance, talk to friends and sometimes swim. One night, we decided to go swimming and while I was changing into my suit, the other girls quietly sneaked out of the dressing room. I searched for them in the pool area and in the dressing room, and then, finally realizing that they had left me, I changed back into my clothes. I then walked the whole building looking for them and called their phones several times. I was beginning to worry that they had left the Rec Center altogether without me.

When I finally found them dancing, I asked, "Why did you leave me?"

"We decided that we didn't want to swim," Riley answered, very nonchalant.

"Yeah, we changed our minds," Erin added.

"You could have told me," I said. "I've been looking all over for you guys for the last half hour. Why didn't you answer your phone?"

Riley shrugged, rolled her eyes and danced closer to the other two girls. When I would start to dance with them, they would turn their backs toward me and dance in a circle facing each other. This happened several times before they abruptly stopped dancing and walked away. I followed and tried to walk next to them, but the three of them locked their arms together, making it apparent that I was not a welcomed part of the group.

I felt excluded again and my feelings were hurt but I was too embarrassed to say anything, so I called my mom and asked her to pick me up early. I lied and told her I wasn't feeling well because I didn't want her to know what had really happened. These were my friends and if I told my mom how they were treating me, she might not have let me hang out with them anymore. I didn't want that to happen.

When I told Riley, Erin and Chelsea that I was leaving, they said goodbye and then I heard Riley mumble under her breath, "thank God."

My stomach twisted into knots, as I knew her comment was directed at me, but I didn't know why. I must have done something to make them mad at me, but I didn't know what.

I laid in bed that night pondering what had happened and trying to justify their actions.

Surely they didn't ditch me in the dressing room on purpose, I told myself. *It was a simple mistake.*

They weren't intentionally blocking me from dancing with them, I told myself. *I'm being too sensitive.*

So they didn't loop my arm with theirs while we were walking. That doesn't mean anything, I tried to console myself.

Riley probably wasn't referring to me when she said, 'thank God', I convinced myself. *We're friends. She wouldn't do that.*

> **People who are being bullied make excuses for the bully's behavior,**

blaming themselves, especially when the bully is perceived as a friend.

It's my fault because I'm too sensitive. I'm too annoying. They didn't mean to exclude me. I just probably misunderstood what they had said. It was an accident. They just forgot. They didn't mean to hurt my feelings. I need to get over it.

These were some of the many excuses I made for them.

That following Monday at school, the girls acted like nothing had happened, so I didn't bring it up. I was afraid that if I said something, they would get mad at me and we'd no longer be friends. At lunch that day they were talking about how they had had a sleepover at Chelsea's house after they had left the Rec Center. I felt a little hurt that they didn't invite me and that must have shown on my face because Erin blurted, "We would have asked you to come but you went home sick."

She was right. I had gone home sick, but I went home because of the way they were treating me. Had they not excluded me, I wouldn't have pretended to be sick and gone home and then I would have gotten to go to the sleepover. It was my fault that I missed out on it…or so I believed at the time.

Bullying victims often feel that it is easier to blame themselves than to point a finger at their friends and risk losing the friendship.

> ➢ **Bullying starts with subtle, little things, but the little things quickly grow into more deliberate, meaner and bigger things.**

Two weeks later my mom drove me and Riley to the Rec Center for Kids Night Out. Chelsea and Erin weren't able to go that night. As we were getting out of the car, my mom said, "Be sure you girls stay together." She always reminded us to stay together. Safety in numbers is one of my mom's many mottos.

"We will," I promised as Riley and I hopped out of the car.

Less than an hour into the night Riley ditched me and, once again, I walked all over the Rec Center, trying to find her. I called Riley's phone a bunch of times but she never answered. I asked other kids if they had seen her and no one seemed to know her whereabouts. I was headed to the front desk to see if they could page her over the intercom when my mom called me on my cell. "Hello?" I answered.

"Where ARE you?" My mom hollered into the phone. She was obviously upset.

"I'm at the Rec Center. Why? What's wrong?" I responded.

"Who are you with?" My mom demanded.

"No one," I answered. "I lost Riley and I've been looking for her for the past hour."

"Riley just called me and told me that you ditched her and went off with two boys and she's been looking all over for you!" My mom yelled and I could tell she was really mad.

"What?!" I exclaimed. "I'm not with any boys! I've been looking for Riley the whole time!"

I couldn't believe it. Riley had ditched me and then called my mom and lied to her trying to get me into trouble. Why would she do that?

"I'm on my way to get you," my mom barked. "Find Riley and be waiting by the front doors."

I never did find Riley that night. When my mom arrived to pick us up and I told her I couldn't find Riley, she went to the front desk and found out that Riley had signed out shortly after my mom had dropped us off. When my mom called Riley's house to make sure she had made it home safely, we were told that Riley's mom had picked her up and dropped her off at Chelsea's house where she and Erin were having a sleepover.

Another sleepover to which I hadn't been invited.

I had been ditched and excluded again, but this time on top of ditching me Riley had lied about me and tried to get me into trouble with my mom. What had I done to deserve this treatment?

"Why would Riley lie to me and leave without telling you?" My mom asked me on the drive home.

"I don't know," I sighed.

"Well, that doesn't sound like much of a friend to me," my mom said with a mixture of disappointment and anger etched across her face.

"No!" I blurted, feeling suddenly compelled to defend Riley so that I could still hang out with her. "No, I probably just misunderstood what she said. There were a lot of people and it was loud and she probably said she was leaving but I didn't realize she meant that she was leaving for good."

My mom shook her head. "That still doesn't explain why she called me and said you had gone off with two boys."

I didn't have a good defense for that statement either, so I just sat quietly, staring out the window. When we got home I went straight to my room and tried to call Riley again, but she didn't answer. She didn't respond to my text messages either. I crawled into bed with questions bouncing around my head. What had I done to make her mad at me again?

Then, I got on Instagram to see videos posted by Chelsea or Erin and Riley dancing around. Chelsea's caption was, "These girls make me so happy."

In the comments, Riley typed, "I'm happy to have loser-free night."

Chelsea added, "Yeah, so glad we didn't have to invite her. Lol"

Even though they never mentioned my name, I knew deep down that they were talking about me. And it hurt. It hurt so bad that I cried myself to sleep.

~

On Monday at school when I asked Riley about what happened at the Rec Center, she told me that someone had told her that they saw me with two older boys and she was worried about me so she called my mom.

"Then why didn't you try to find me?" I asked.

"I didn't want to interrupt whatever it was that you were doing," she said with accusation in her tone.

"I wasn't talking to any boys!" I rebutted.

"I didn't say you were *talking* with them," she quipped, raising her eyebrows with a snide grin, insinuating for the second time that I had done something inappropriate.

"I spent the whole night looking for you," I said.

"That's not what I heard," she chided and then strode down the hall, joining Chelsea and Erin. She said something to them and then they looked over their shoulders and laughed at me.

Why would Riley lie about me? I hadn't done anything wrong. And what had she said to Chelsea and Erin to make them laugh at me? Did they believe that I had gone off with two older boys and done something bad? How could they think that?

> **I hadn't done anything wrong and yet, somehow, they made me feel ashamed.**

Tactics of exclusion, rumor spreading, talking behind my back, telling secrets in front of me and saying things to me and about me that made me feel bad about myself became the norm, and as hurtful as these things were, they were still so subtle that if I told anyone they would have seemed trivial and unimportant. So, I kept quiet.

> ## **Bullying chips away at your self-esteem**
> **one comment at a time.**

"Maya, someone like you shouldn't wear a shirt like that. You don't look good," Riley said one day at school and I felt awkward and self-conscious the rest of the day. "I'm just trying to help you," she justified. "That's what friends do."

That's what friends do, I repeated the phrase in my mind. *That's what friends do,* she had said. *So, that must mean we are still friends,* I rationalized.

There was a dress code at our school. Plain colored, collared shirts on the top and either navy, khaki or black pants, shorts or skirt on the bottom. The collared shirt I was wearing when she made her comment was no different from what everyone else was wearing. It was a light pink, short-sleeved, polo-style shirt. The only difference was that it was on me.

That night I went home and tried on all of my collared shirts. Riley was right. They didn't look good on me. So, to compensate for not looking good in the dress code shirts, I began to add scarves to my wardrobe repertoire. I thought this worked pretty well until one day I overheard Erin say to Chelsea, "Even a scarf can't hide her marshmallow arms."

Erin laughed and Chelsea added, "Yeah, a scarf can't fix fat and ugly."

I called my mom and asked her to bring me a sweater. I didn't tell her it was to hide my "marshmallow arms." I lied and told her I was freezing in my classes.

From that point forward, I kept a sweater in my locker. I didn't wear short sleeves without a sweater over the top for the rest of that year, even when it was ninety degrees outside. I didn't want anyone to see my "marshmallow arms."

This became the norm. Every day I was verbally cut down by one of the girls. They made fun of my clothes, my bangs, my body, my skin, my teeth, everything. A lot of the time it was under the guise of "helping me" not "making fun of me," but the helping hurt. Their words sliced like a knife right through my self-esteem. They hurt my feelings and worse yet, they made me feel ashamed until all I wanted to do was crawl into a hole and stay there.

> **Words are powerful. They can never be un-said or un-heard and the damage they cause can last forever.**

Despite the fact that they had hurt my feelings on numerous occasions, we still sat together at lunch, because in my mind we were still friends. Riley had said it herself. *"That's what friends do."* Friends are supposed to be honest with each other and so I told myself that Riley was only trying to help me by telling me that I looked bad in the collared shirts. I justified every mean thing they said to me as them simply trying to help me look better and be better.

Real friends are honest and truthful but not in a way that embarrasses or humiliates. If an outfit doesn't look good on you, a real friend won't blurt out how disgusting you look. Instead, they might mention how a particular style would flatter you more. Real friends uplift through positive criticisms. They don't continually tear you down. Bullies do.

> **Bullying victims often justify the mean things that are said to them by so-called "friends" because they think it's better to have friends who are painfully honest than have no friends at all.**

Mid-way through our six grade year they stopped pretending to be my friend and started deliberately striking out to hurt me. Suddenly, they had gone from friend status to frenemies and were now headed down the path toward becoming enemies.

I didn't know what I had done to lose their friendship, but whatever it was, I was sorry. I was so sorry and all I wanted was for them to forgive me and for things to go back to the way they were in the beginning.

> **Bullying victims often apologize to the bully because they truly believe they have done something to deserve to be bullied.**

One afternoon when I sat down at our lunch table, Riley whispered something to Chelsea, they laughed and then they got up and moved to another table. Erin tried not to laugh, lowered her eyes to the floor, mumbled quietly that she was sorry and then quickly left and joined the others.

I picked up my tray and followed them but the moment I sat down at the new table, all three of them got up and moved again, leaving me sitting alone.

I was too afraid that if I followed them a second time that they'd get up and leave again, so, I text Riley instead.

IS THIS A JOKE? I texted and as soon as I pressed SEND I heard them all burst into laughter.

"What a loser," Chelsea said loud enough that I could hear her.

UR A JOKE! Riley texted back and they all laughed again.

I can't describe what I felt at that moment. At first, I thought it was a prank, like I was being punked or something. Then, as the realization settled in that it wasn't a joke, that the only joke was me, my heart sank. I felt embarrassed, humiliated, degraded, unworthy and disgusting. Why else would they do this to me unless I deserved it?

I tried to talk to them in the hallway after lunch, but they ignored me. I tried to tell them that I was sorry for whatever I did to make them hate me, but they wouldn't listen. Other than Riley rolling her eyes at me, they acted as if I wasn't even there.

> **I didn't understand what was happening or what I had done to deserve it.**

The next day I mustered up the courage to try to join them at the lunch table again and Chelsea said I couldn't sit there.

I asked why and Riley said, "This is OUR table." Clearly letting me know that I was no longer considered part of the "our." I was officially no longer one of them.

> **When you're bullied it becomes quickly clear that you are not good enough to be a part of a group. You're the outsider, the outcast, the one who deserves to be all alone.**

From that point forward that's what I was…alone. Day after day, lunch after lunch, I sat alone while they made fun of me from several tables away. Every once in a while they would look over at me and then whisper to each other and laugh. They made it obvious that they were talking about me. They wanted me to know that they were making fun of me, and that I was a joke to them.

> **Being bullied is humiliating.**

Any middle schooler will tell you that lunch and recess are the highlights of the day, but not for me. For me, they had become the worst part of my day because without fail, Riley, Chelsea and Erin would go out of their way during lunch and recess to be mean to me.

I couldn't avoid going to recess, so I started taking a book with me and sitting alone against the far wall, pretending to read. I figured if I just stayed out of their way, they'd be less inclined to harass me. Sometimes it worked and they would leave me alone. Other days, they'd stand close enough for me to overhear their conversation and they'd say mean things about me.

One day, while standing close to where I was sitting, Chelsea mentioned the name of a boy that they knew I liked. Remember, we had been friends so they knew my secrets and my crushes. I had had a crush on this particular boy for a while but had never told him. Chelsea said to Riley, "Didn't you talk to Nathan about Maya?"

I wasn't trying to eavesdrop but my ears perked up at the mention of his name and mine.

"Oh, yeah, I did," said Riley. "I asked if he liked her."

"What did he say?" Erin questioned.

Riley laughed. "He said she was too gross to date."

And then they paraded away, giggling together at my expense. Hiding behind the pages of my book, I wilted.

Lunch became a daily torture until I finally just stopped going. We weren't allowed to be in the halls during lunch period so I hid in the bathroom. If I heard someone coming in, I'd rush into a stall and hide until they left. You see, in the bathroom stall, nobody could hurt me because nobody knew I was there. It was the one place I was safe.

But, have you ever tried to eat in a public bathroom? It's gross. Then again, according to Nathan, I was obviously gross so somehow it seemed fitting.

> ➢ **When you're bullied you learn fast that it hurts less to be invisible than it does to be seen. In fact, you start to wish you really were invisible. If they can't see you, they can't hurt you.**

I later learned that Riley had never even asked Nathan about me and Nathan had never called me gross. Riley had made it all up simply to hurt me and she succeeded...for a time.

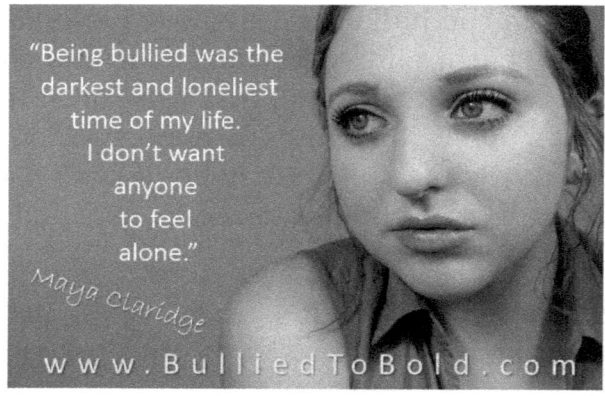

Picture courtesy of WTManagement
© 2016 Global Publishing Group LLC

CHAPTER TWO

THE YO-YO EFFECT

Every once in a while, as middle school girls do, Erin, Chelsea and Riley would get mad at each other. They'd get into a fight and then one of them would come to me and all of a sudden I would find myself back in the group. They would tell me secrets, spend the night and sit with me at lunch.

I'd be lying if I said I didn't look forward to them fighting because when one of them ran to me, it meant that I was no longer alone; and that felt really, really good.

But as quickly as they got into fights, they made up and the moment their conflict was resolved, I was dumped again. This happened over and over and over. I was in the group, then kicked out, then back in, then kicked out and I felt like a yo-yo.

Looking back I realize how they used me, but in the moment, when I was so lonely, I couldn't see what was happening.

One time Riley got in a fight with Chelsea and Erin and out of the blue Riley began acting like I was her best friend. She came over my house and told me all of the horrible things Chelsea and Erin had said about me. Terrible things. It hurt my feelings and it made me angry. In retaliation, I said some awful things about Chelsea and Erin that night, things that I didn't even mean. Things I just wanted to move on from, but Riley recorded our conversation. That following Monday she played the recording for Chelsea and Erin and a lot of other people at school and told everyone that I was "the bitch who was badmouthing them." She also accused me of trying to sabotage her friendship with Chelsea and Erin.

Had Riley staged the whole fight with Chelsea and Erin just to come over my house and set me up to look bad in front of everyone at school? Was she that clever? Did they all plan it?

That's when I began to realize that every time they pulled me in and then kicked me out, their words grew harsher and their actions meaner and more deliberate. Thanks to the recording Riley had made, it was no longer just them against me; they were rallying others to hate me as well.

> **It wasn't just that they didn't want to be my friend, it was that they didn't want me to have any friends.**

I walked down the hall toward my first hour class and a boy named James said sarcastically, "Way to be a bitch, Maya."

What could I say? I had no defense. The truth was that I had said those things about Chelsea and Erin, but I only said them to Riley because she had told me all of the horrible things that they had said about me first. Still, I had said them and there was no denying that fact.

After first hour I approached the three girls at Chelsea's locker. "I'm sorry for what I said," I told them. "Riley told me what you guys had said about me and I was mad and I'm sorry."

"Don't listen to her," Riley blurted. "She's just trying to leach onto us to be popular, and she never will be."

"Her? Popular? What a joke," Chelsea muttered and Erin said nothing.

And that's exactly what I felt like…a joke. I wasn't after popularity. I mean, sure everyone wants to be popular but we all realize that not everyone can carry that title. Right, wrong or indifferently popularity is reserved for the chosen few, of which I was not one. All I really wanted was to stop hurting, to be accepted for who I was and to have friends that didn't treat me like I was a yo-yo.

> **Them befriending and unfriending me became a vicious cycle that lasted years. It was a cycle I didn't know how to break and it left me broken.**

In an attempt to try and win their friendship back, I threw a Halloween party at my house and invited everyone in our class. I love Halloween! I love the costumes and the decorations and the spooky treats and so does my mom, which is why she went all out helping me set up for the perfect Halloween bash. The entire house was covered in webs with decorations galore. We had tons of food and my mom had wired strobe lights and party laser lights in every room. I was hopeful that once Riley, Chelsea and Erin saw how cool my party was, they would want to be friends again. I was hoping that everyone would see that I wasn't a mean person after all.

I was excited when they RSVP'd that they were coming to the party. What I didn't realize was that the only reason they had agreed to come was to make fun of me.

"She looks so fat in that costume!" Erin hollered across the room, as if she was hollering over the music, but it was really so that everyone would hear and I would be humiliated.

"And her bangs are so ugly!" Chelsea added and I felt my face flush with embarrassment.

They didn't stay long. They had just shown up and stayed long enough to make me feel bad. As they were leaving, Riley said, "We're going to go sleep over at my house." It was her way of rubbing in my face the fact that I was not invited...again.

"This party is lame," Chelsea added as they walked out the front door.

Needless to say, after the three most popular girls left the party it didn't take long for the other guests to follow suit. When my mom asked why everyone had gone home early, I felt suddenly enraged and screamed at her, as if it was her fault, though I knew it wasn't. "Because the party was boring! It sucked!"

"What?" My mom was puzzled. "Why did it suck?"

"Just forget it! It was a stupid idea!" I screamed and rushed to my room.

My mom was upset with me because she thought I had an ungrateful attitude for everything we had spent and done to make the party extra-special. She thought I was being a brat and I let her think it because that was easier than telling her what was really going on.

~

The following week I was standing at my locker chatting with another girl about a homework assignment. She was someone I knew from class but we weren't friends. We were barely what you'd call acquaintances. Riley, Chelsea and Erin approached us and Chelsea said to this girl, "Why are hanging out with that loser?"

"Are you trying to commit social suicide?" Riley asked.

"If anyone should commit suicide, we all know who that should be," Erin said and then glared at me, smirking.

I could feel a lump rise in my throat and Erin must have seen that I was fighting back tears because she looked at me and said, "Lighten up, Maya, we're just joking."

And then, as they walked away Riley muttered beneath her breath, "Not!"

Even before she said "Not" I knew that they weren't joking. I knew that they wouldn't care if I was dead.

> **Bullies will often try to play their words off as if they are joking…but telling someone to kill themselves is no joke.**

The classmate I had been talking to at the locker didn't say anything. She just sort of awkwardly turned her back toward me and hurried away. I wasn't sure which was more painful in that moment, what had been said to me by the bullies or the fact that their words and actions had been justified by a third party. I couldn't expect that girl to defend me. She didn't even know me, not really; and, yet, she allowed them to harass me. Her silence gave them permission. Her silence told me that she was in agreement with them, that she saw no error in their words and that she felt there was no reason to speak up on my behalf.

It was as if she loaded the gun and handed it to the bully to pull the trigger.

> **Her silence confirmed in my mind that the bullies were right about me. I was better off dead.**

There are no innocent bystanders when it comes to bullying. There are only three roles in bullying. The bully. The target. The bystander. According to the CDC over seventy percent (70%) of young people (grades 6th-12th) have witnessed someone being bullied.

> **If you witness someone being bullied and you do nothing to stop it, you are an active participant in the abuse.**

CHAPTER THREE

CYBER-BULLYING

Social media has made it easy for people to express their negative thoughts toward others behind the safety of a screen. It allows anyone to pass judgment on another person without having to face that person and see the damage their words have caused.

It also robs the victim of a safe haven because the internet stretches far beyond the hallways, the blacktop and the lunchroom at school, allowing the cyber-bully's tentacles to reach into the victim's home.

In the olden days, the days before social media, the bully could do nothing more to you once you were in the sanctity of your home. There was safety there. Social media has stripped away that security, as even laying under the covers in your bedroom the bully still holds the power.

> **Forty-two percent (42%) of teenagers with social media access report being cyber-bullied in the past year.**
> (Statistics from Cyberbullying hotline research)

> **Twenty percent (20%) of kids who are cyberbullied think about committing suicide. One in every ten attempt it.**
> (Statistics from Cyberbullying hotline research)

Beneath pictures on my Instagram, they would comment, calling me "a waste of space" and various other names, like fat, ugly, stupid, weird, worthless, loser and a joke. They would write "everyone hates you" and "you should go away." There were more names, but you get the gist. They would make fun of my hair, my face, my teeth, my weight, my body and my clothes. Comment by comment, they would dismantle my self-esteem.

Quiet consistency is the underlying power in bullying. A bully doesn't say something one time or pick on a person one day. They say it ten times every day via every avenue available until you begin to realize that there is no escape.

> ➢ **Over time you start to believe the things they say about you. You begin to lose yourself in their words. And it finally gets to a point where when you look in the mirror you only see what they have told you to see.**

It got to a point where all I saw when I stared at my reflection was a fat, ugly, worthless, waste of space.

For me, the torture didn't stop there…

I was told about events and then not invited at all or worse yet, invited and then uninvited. Then, they would post pictures and videos on social media and tag me so that they were sure that I saw that I had been excluded. They'd comment things like, "SO glad the loser isn't here!"

I would read the comments alone in my room and cry.

> **Cyber bullying feels like you're being punched in the stomach over and over because every time you read and re-read the hateful comments, it hurts again and again and again.**

And you find yourself obsessing about the comments and how many people have *liked* something the bully has said about you. You keep checking, hoping someone will defend you, and when they don't you begin to feel as if the whole world is against you.

> **Words hurt. Words destroy. Words can kill.**

CHAPTER FOUR

POISON TO THE SOUL IS DEADLY TO THE BODY

This consistent, mean behavior went on for over two years. I dreaded walking down the halls at school because they'd talk about me, look over their shoulders at me and laugh. I'd hear them say things about me, calling me names, but I learned to just keep walking. Their taunting and harassment was getting old and they were running out of new things to say about me.

One of their favorite things to harass me about was my skin. I have pale skin. Like, porcelain pale skin. I have to buy the fairest of the fair base and powder make-up and even those are too dark. Riley, Erin and Chelsea used to be ruthless about my pale skin.

"Look how white she is!" Riley would mock.

To which Chelsea would add, "It's gross."

"Hey, Maya, do you EVER see the sun?" Erin would say and then they'd all three laugh.

Sometimes Riley would say I looked like a vampire, which I would later, upon becoming an avid Vampire Diaries fan, learn to take as a compliment.

On occasion while making fun of my skin color, one of them would remark that I looked sickly. Looking back I find this ironic because I was sick all of the time.

At first, I would pretend to be sick so that I didn't have to go to school and face these girls. The problem was that this didn't always work. Often times my mom would take me to the doctor and when the doctor found nothing wrong with me, my mom would make me go to school.

Over time, I hated myself so much that it actually made me physically sick. I didn't realize it at the time but the depression I was experiencing from being bullied had begun to manifest itself physically. My head always hurt and I was constantly nauseous. My body ached all over, like when you have the flu. I was lethargic and felt tired all of the time but had difficulty staying asleep. This was mainly because I would have nightmares related to the emotional stress I was under. The more sleep deprived I became, the lower my energy and the lower my energy, the greater my hopelessness, as I saw no end in sight.

> **Three (3) million kids per month are absent from school due to bullying.**
> (Statistics from Cyberbullying hotline research)

My parents would make me go to school and I'd end up going to the school nurse and asking her to call my mom and send me home. The nurse would roll her eyes and give an exasperated sigh every time I came to her office. She was sick of seeing me and I was sick of being there. My teachers grew irritated. My parents grew frustrated. No one knew what to do with me, including me.

> ### **It became a vicious cycle that I didn't have the strength to break because I was broken.**

The District sent truancy letters to my parents and they met with my Principal, trying to explain why I was missing so much school. But it was hard to justify when the doctors couldn't find anything wrong with me. I was tested for every allergy, via thirty-two pin pricks on my back and even went gluten-free to see if that would lessen my symptoms. Nothing worked because the only thing I was allergic to was those three girls.

I fell behind on my school work and fought to make myself work harder. I wanted good grades. I wanted my teachers to know that school was important to me. I just didn't want to face the bullies and be ridiculed and abused every day.

One day my math teacher said in front of the whole class, "Maya obviously doesn't care about school." I was devastated because I did care. I really did care.

> **It felt like everything was spiraling out of control and I just wanted it all to stop. I wanted the pain to stop.**

I cried every morning that I had to go to school and every day after school. My parents didn't know what was happening and I didn't know how to tell them. I was trapped by fear.

> **It was the darkest and loneliest time of my life.**

A bully's words are poisonous to the soul. Over time that poison negatively affects the body and the mind.

CHAPTER FIVE

WHY ARE YOU EVEN HERE?

When the exclusion, name calling, the cyber bullying and the constant harassment wasn't enough, Riley, Chelsea and Erin spread rumors about me. They actually told lies about me, telling everyone at school that I had done or said things that I had never done or said. They destroyed my reputation and made our classmates believe that I was a "bitch" and a bad person.

I tried to disprove the rumors, but I could feel the condescending stares of my peers from across the classrooms and in the hallways. I had no way of defending myself. It was their word against mine. There were three of them all corroborating whatever lie they thought up. And they were pretty and popular and everybody listened to them, liked them and believed them. I was nobody and no one believes a nobody.

They not only stripped me of their so-called friendship, but they worked hard to ensure that I would have no friends.

One day I mustered up the courage to ask Riley why she said bad things about me. Her answer was this: "I only speak the truth and the bad things are true."

The humiliation and the constant embarrassment I felt became overwhelming. It was more than I could explain to anyone, or even understand myself, so I eventually just stopped trying. Because by now the answer had become obvious: They were right about me. I was a fat, ugly, worthless loser who everyone hated.

> **All of those names, those labels that the bullies had said stuck to me, became a part of me...and then...they became all of me.**

I grew weaker and they grew stronger. "Accidentally" pushing me against lockers, tripping me, purposefully knocking books out of my hands, laughing at me. These things became a regular occurrence.

One day, as I stood in front of my open locker, reaching for a folder, the girls walked by. I turned my back to them in hopes that they would pass by without saying anything or doing anything to me. I was praying to be invisible in that moment.

"God, Maya, why are you even here?" Erin sneered as they passed by.

Why are you even here? Why are you even here? I repeated the phrase over and over in my mind trying to find the answer. Why was I here? With tears streaming down my cheeks I rushed into the bathroom and stood there, staring blankly at my reflection; Erin's words replaying in my mind. *Why are you even here?*

> ➤ **"I don't want to be here anymore," I whispered.**

I wanted that reflection to disappear. I wanted to smash it. I wanted to kill it. I wanted to cut it out of me. I wanted to make it go away. But mostly, I just wanted the pain to stop. I would have done anything to make the pain stop.

It's at this point when many kids start cutting because they want to feel anything other than the heartache. They want to cut the pain out of themselves. They want to feel something other than the constant emotional hurt, the sadness and the emptiness. A slice on the skin is less painful than the knives penetrating their heart.

This is often the point when kids choose suicide. It isn't because they want to hurt their loved ones. It isn't because they don't love their families. It's because they truly believe everyone would be better off without them. It's because they believe they are a worthless burden to everyone around them. It's because they can't go another day hurting.

It's because they are rendered immobile by the fear that they will feel this way for the rest of their lives.

"When you're being bullied
you can't see yourself clearly.
Your self-image blurs.
Your self-esteem becomes distorted.
Your self-confidence fades.
And you find yourself wanting
to disappear altogether."
Maya Claridge

Stop the Hate
before it's too late

www.BulliedToBold.com

CHAPTER SIX

EXTERNAL VERSUS INTERNAL PAIN

If someone punches you in the face, everyone can see your black eye and they know that you've been hurt. They show concern for you by asking, "Oh, wow, what happened to your eye?" Or, "Are you okay?" They talk with you about how it happened because they can see proof of your pain.

External pain warrants the attention of others.

Being bullied is like being punched on the inside and it leaves bruises that no one can see. And when no one can see that you're hurting, no one asks how you are doing. When no one asks how you are doing or notices that you are hurting, you start to feel that much more invisible, meaningless and worthless; and you start to believe that nobody cares.

"Nobody sees me hurting so that means that nobody cares about me." That's what we tell ourselves. But that's not the truth. The truth is people can't see internal wounds like they can the external ones, but the internal ones are often times the most painful and take the longest to heal.

> **Being punched in the face hurts, but being bullied kills.**

According to the CDC, suicide has become the third leading cause of death in young people. 4,400 people, ages 10-24 years, commit suicide every year. For every one of those, 100 people attempt it. A huge percentage of that is due to some form of bullying.

In fact, statistically every person in a school classroom has either been bullied, seen someone being bullied or are guilty of bullying.

We have to stop this from happening. We have to **Stop the Hate Before it's too Late**. We owe it to ourselves, to our friends and to our families.

How do we do that? We have to drain the bully's fuel and remove his or her power.

Picture courtesy of WTManagement
© 2016 Global Publishing Group LLC

CHAPTER SEVEN

A BULLY'S FUEL

Have you ever wondered why bullying is so hard to stop? There are several reasons. First, because bullies are smart.

The reality is, and I'm sure most of you reading this already know, bullies aren't going to bully anyone in front of their teachers or principals or parents or any other adult. What they do is quiet. It's subtle. It's behind the scenes. It's underhanded. It's passive-aggressive. It's cunning. It's silent. It's a look. An expression. A stare. A laugh. A hard nudge with their shoulder as they pass by. It's a text. It's a comment on a photo that is then deleted. It's a snapchat video that disappears after the damage is done. It's a sentence uttered almost in silence with the power of an Atomic bomb.

Bullies aren't stupid. They play nice in front of others and then stab you when no one else is watching.

So, the question becomes, if adults can't see the bully bullying someone how can they stop them? The real answer is, and they won't want to admit this, but they can't. Unless they witness the bullying firsthand, adults are powerless to stop it from happening.

Pre-Teens and Teens, this is our battlefield and we must stop it ourselves.

We'd all like to believe that Taylor Swift's song is right; that haters are gonna hate and all we have to do is shake it off. Unfortunately, that doesn't work when you're being bullied. Over time, when the bully's words and actions have sunk into you, destroyed your self-esteem, your self-worth and who you believe you are, you can't just shake it off. It won't go away. You can't pick up a blade and CUT it out of you.

The only answer is to eliminate the bully's fuel. We can stop the bully by removing his or her source of power.

Bullies thrive on one thing: FEAR

Hundreds of Anti-Bullying organizations will tell you that the first thing you should do if you are being bullied is ask for help. They are right, you do need to ask for help, but that's not the first thing you do. You see, when fear has enslaved you into silence for so long, you cannot possibly imagine even verbalizing what is happening much less asking for help.

There were countless times when I would lie in my bed and wish I could tell my parents what was really going on, but I didn't know how. Where would I start? What would they say? What if they didn't believe me? What if they got mad at me? Wouldn't telling them just cause stress in our home and in our family? Remember, when you're being bullied you believe that it's your fault, that you have somehow caused all of it. I was afraid my parents would blame me the way I was blaming myself. I never spoke up because I was literally silenced by fear.

The first thing you have to do is PUT DOWN YOUR FEAR.

> **Your fear is the source of the bully's power.**
> **You have to PUT DOWN your fear in order to stop the bully.**

It is hard for me to describe the fear that bullying causes. It's deafening. It's all-controlling. It is strong. It is scary. It is over-powering. It forces the victim into silence. I was terrified to tell anyone what was happening because I thought that no one would believe me, and I didn't know what would happen then. If no one believed me then there would be no hope for me. I was too afraid to face the possibility of absolute hopelessness.

> **When you can't outwardly prove that you are being bullied, you become silenced by the fear that no one will believe you.**

Bullies count on this... silence. It fuels them. It protects them. I can't count the number of times Riley said to me, "Nobody will ever believe you, Maya." Her words grew fear in me and that fear caused me to go silent.

> ➢ **Silence empowers bullies.**

More frightening than the prospect of not being believed was the fear that if I told someone what was happening, that things would get worse. I was imprisoned by this fear for over two years. *What will they do to me if I tell?* That was all I could think about and it made me physically nauseated.

> ➢ **The fear that things will get worse is suffocating.**

But, let me pose one question, a question you have to dig down deep and ask yourself: How much worse can it get? When you're staring at the mirror, hating what you see, wanting to disappear from the face of the earth... what's worse than that?

When your chest aches and you feel like you can't breathe...

When you cut your own flesh just to watch it bleed...

When you hate who you are and wish you were dead...

When thoughts of disappearing are all that are in your head...

What could be worse than that?

What could be worse?

The answer is nothing. Nothing could be worse. If you are at a breaking point, feeling as if the only way to stop the pain is to hurt yourself or kill yourself, then there is nothing more a bully can do to destroy you.

Think about this for a moment. You have nothing to lose. That is a powerful position. The bully has stripped you of everything and yet, you are still here. That means you are not a quitter. You are not a vulnerable victim that has to allow another person to destroy your life. You are at a crossroads, not a dead end. You can choose to put down the fear and take back your power.

> **PUT DOWN YOUR FEAR because when you do, the bully loses power and you gain it.**

CHAPTER EIGHT

STEP ONE: PUT DOWN YOUR FEAR

I don't want to make light of this because it's not an easy step. When you are bullied for a long time, the fear becomes part of you. It implants inside of you. It changes you. It makes you reclusive and untrusting. So, to put it down can feel as if you are ripping out a piece of your soul. It's hard. But if you can endure years of constant harassment, belittlement and humiliation, then you are a strong person and you can take this step.

PUT DOWN YOUR FEAR and tell someone that you are being bullied. It doesn't matter who you tell at first. It only matters that you verbalize what is happening.

Breaking that silence was one of the most freeing feelings I've ever experienced. It will free you, too. The moment the words left my lips a huge weight felt like it was lifted off of my shoulders and my chest. All of a sudden, I was no longer alone and I didn't have to face this alone anymore.

The first person I told was my mom. I cried. She cried. She got angry, not at me, but at the girls who were bullying me and at all of the bystanders who did nothing to help me. Telling my mom wasn't easy because there was so much self-blame and shame. I felt like I was confessing to doing something wrong... when the truth was that I had done nothing wrong.

> ➤ **People who are bullied blame themselves, believing they have caused the problem... "If I was different this wouldn't be happening."**

But my mom helped me to see that bullying is an injustice, that no one deserves it nor could do anything to deserve it; and that the blame fell squarely on the bully's shoulders.

The next person I told was my school Principal. That was harder than telling my mom because I was scared to death that the Principal would not believe me. After all, I was accusing the three most popular girls in our grade of bullying. I'll never forget how my hands were trembling as I walked into the office and asked to speak with the Principal. My heart was pounding fiercely in my chest and I was praying that I wouldn't burst into tears before I even got a word out. But as scared as I was, I knew this was the only way to overcome the pain.

> ➢ **People who are being bullied know deep down that even scarier than telling is NOT telling because continuing to live the way they are living is no longer an option in their mind.**

> **They want the pain to stop no matter what it takes to stop it. This is a dangerous crossroads where the fear is so strong that it causes too many bullied kids to choose suicide over confiding in someone.**

PUT DOWN the fear.

My principal called the three girls and me into her office and she confronted them with the information I had given her. They looked the principal right in the eyes and lied. I don't know why that shocked me, but it did. After all of the lies they had told about me, I should have expected them to lie to her, but somehow it still came as a surprise. They told her I was just trying to get them into trouble. They said I was jealous of them and told her that I had been saying bad things about them. Riley even offered to play the recorded message of me saying bad things about Chelsea and Erin; but I had already told the Principal about that recording and how it was made.

Still, as I sat there, fear filled me and I felt like I was going to vomit. I started to panic, thinking I had just made everything worse. Fear told me that the Principal would never believe me over these three, popular girls. *You are nothing compared to them! You're going to be expelled now! The Principal is going to hate you, just like everyone else does!* Fear taunted me and tears formed in my eyes.

She dismissed the girls and then turned to me and I thought I was in trouble. But instead, she handed me a Kleenex and said, "Maya, I believe you and we're going to fix this."

I can't describe to you what it felt like to hear her say those words. "I believe you." She may not have seen the actual bullying take place... but she could now see the bruises on the inside of me...she could see the internal pain that I had been hiding for so long.

> ➢ **In that moment, in that very instant, I was no longer invisible. I was no longer alone.**

STEP ONE – Putting Down Your Fear and Breaking the Silence

Step one is not asking for help, it's <u>putting down</u> your fear... the fear of not being believed...the fear of being blamed...the fear that things will get worse if you tell...

PUT IT DOWN and allow someone to see what is happening to you.

~

Now, I know what you're thinking. You're thinking, "But Maya, I've gone to my teachers and my parents and the Principal and nobody has done anything about it!"

I know. Putting down your fear and telling someone doesn't mean that the bullying will stop, at least not right away. But the reason you tell isn't to get it to stop, it's to be seen, to empower yourself by breaking the silence and overcoming the fear. It also lets the bully know that you're no longer going to lie down and take whatever they dish out. It lets the bully know that you are going to fight back.

It's hard for adults to stop something that they don't see happening. And because they can't fix things immediately, we start to think they can't fix them at all. But that isn't true.

> ➢ **When you tell someone what's happening, it's not to get them to stop it from happening, at least not immediately...it's to get someone in your corner...someone who believes you...someone who can help strengthen you.**
>
> **Because as you grow stronger, the bully grows weaker.**

Remember, bullies are empowered by your silence. The moment you PUT DOWN your fear and speak up, they lose their power over you. As you speak, they begin to become silenced and the fear changes hands, as you become less afraid of them and they now become afraid of getting caught.

CHAPTER NINE

STEP TWO:
BUILD A SUPPORT SYSTEM

Once you have put down your fear and broken your silence, your next step is to develop a support system.

A support system can be one person or it can be a handful of people. The important thing is that it is a person or people you trust. What may surprise you is that in doing this you will most like discover that you are not the only person being bullied. Others, just like you, have been internally beaten into silence and imprisoned by fear. When you speak up, you empower them to share their story. You find a common ground and you watch each other's backs, making it more difficult for the bully to engage. Together you begin to put down the heartache and repair the damage.

All of those words that caused you humiliation and sadness... all of those words that caused you to start hating yourself... all of those words that seeped into your heart and made you believe that the bullies were right about you... with the help and strength of a support system, you can PUT THOSE WORDS AND THE PAIN ASSOCIATED WITH THEM, DOWN ONCE AND FOR ALL.

When you have someone in your corner... to remind you...to believe in you... to prove to you that those words aren't true... it strengthens you...and the stronger you become the weaker the bully becomes.

I want to share with you some of those words that I had to dismantle one-by-one in my mind. With the help of my support system, I was able to realize that these names that I had been called for years were inaccurate and made no sense. I was too weak to dismantle and disempower them on my own, but with my support system, I was able to do it and with every word that I put down, I grew stronger.

FAT

So what if I'm not as skinny as Riley, Chelsea and Erin? That doesn't make me less of a person, in fact, more weight technically means I'm more of a person, at least numerically speaking! HA! Everyone is built differently. Some of us are short, some tall, some big, some little. The shape of your body has nothing to do with the worth of your soul. Put that word down.

UGLY

Beauty is in the eye of the beholder, so who is anyone to judge another person? Outward beauty can be subjective, meaning someone you find attractive I may not find attractive and vice versa. Besides, beauty is more than external. True beauty shines from the inside out. I might not look like a Victoria Secret model, but there are beautiful qualities about me...about you...about everyone. Put that word down.

WORTHLESS

How can anyone be worthless when you're the only YOU in the whole wide world? There will never be another you or another me.

That makes us unique, special, a one-of-a-kind and there is nothing more valuable than a one-of-a-kind. So if you think about it, no can be worthless. Put that word down.

WEIRD

This is my favorite. It used to hurt me but I actually take this as a compliment now. Because if someone calls you weird, it only means you're different. So, embrace your differences because some of the most entertaining, likeable, wonderful people in the world were once considered weirdos. Put that word down.

One by one you dismantle their words. You pull their daggers out of your heart and you put them down. Every time a hurtful memory or phrase pops into your mind...and it will happen a thousand times a day... you force yourself to PUT IT DOWN.

See, when you hold onto the bully's words, you give him or her the continual power to hurt you. When you put those words down, you empower yourself to rise above the pain.

> **Words hurt. But they don't define you unless you let them. Don't let them.**

There are hundreds of examples of people who refused to let other people's words define them. These people weren't necessarily bullied but they are great examples of individuals who would not be hindered by the negative opinions of others.

- Dr. Seuss was told that he was a terrible writer and terrible artist.

- Michael Jordan didn't make his high school basketball team and the coach told him that basketball wasn't his sport.

- Walt Disney was fired from his job with the Kansas City Star newspaper because his editor said he "lacked imagination and had no good ideas."

- Elvis Presley was told by his manager that he would be better off driving trucks than singing.

- Albert Einstein was told that he wasn't smart.

- Lucille Ball was told by her acting coaches that she wasn't funny and would never become an actress.

- Marilyn Monroe was told that she was too fat and too ugly to model. She went on to become one of the world's biggest icons.

- Steven Spielberg was rejected from the California School of Film three times, being told he had no film making skills.

- Stephen King's first book was rejected 30 times, one editor telling him he would never be a successful writer.

The point is, other people's opinions of you, don't shape who you are and who you can become. Don't give their words the power to hurt you.

CHAPTER TEN

STEP THREE:
STOP THE BLAME AND SHAME

I call it the "IF Game."

IF I was different... IF I was this or that...IF I was anyone but me...this wouldn't have happened and the bully wouldn't mistreat me. They would like me and we would be friends.

Our minds like to play the "IF Game" and once the game begins it is difficult to stop it. Most of us have a built in justice meter which tells us that someone must take responsibility for behavior, whether good or bad. Someone must be responsible and when the bully consistently blames the victim, the victim over time shoulders that responsibility and the guilt that accompanies it.

➢ **Bullying is an injustice.**

There is no rationalizing it nor justifying it. There is nothing a person can do to deserve to be bullied. So, stop blaming and shaming yourself.

You didn't do anything to deserve to be bullied. It isn't your fault. There's nothing you could have done differently. It isn't fair. It isn't right. You are NOT to blame. The bully is solely responsible for the damage he or she has caused. What they are doing is wrong, hateful and mean. Their hatefulness is no reflection on who you are. It is a reflection on who they are.

Don't play the "IF Game."

CHAPTER ELEVEN

NOTE TO BULLIES

Bullying is a bad behavior but that doesn't necessarily mean that the bully is a bad person. There's a reason why they bully others. Maybe it's because there is pain in they're life. Maybe it's a pain that no one knows about or sees and they feel as invisible as the person they're bullying. Maybe when they bully they feel powerful and that power feels good for a moment. Maybe when they bully they feel seen and accepted. Maybe when they bully they feel less afraid. Or maybe they're just a really mean-spirited person.

Whatever the reason, hurting someone else doesn't heal your own wounds. Shaming others for their weaknesses won't make up for your own inadequacies. Driving someone else to the verge of suicide doesn't improve your life.

A huge percentage of suicide is due to bullying and a high percentage of those who kill themselves are actually the bullies. The deliberate pain they cause in others will eventually catch up to them and it will destroy them.

> **There is no excuse for bullying.**

The good news is that the bullies have the power to change their behavior. A variation of the steps in this book applies to them, too.

Step One: Put down your fear instead of causing fear in others.

Step Two: Put down the hateful and mean words before they leave your mouth and rip someone else apart.

Step Three: Stop blaming and shaming others for your own shortcomings.

Bullies, you cannot change what you've done in the past. You can't take back your words or actions, but you can take responsibility for them. You can apologize. You can take ownership of the damage you have caused and you can treat people differently going forward. You and only you have the power to make that change.

It takes a strong person to change. Isn't it time you stopped pretending to be the strongest and actually started behaving like it.

Stop the Hate Before it's too Late.

CHAPTER TWELVE

NOTE TO THE BYSTANDERS

To those of you who have seen someone being bullied and like the girl standing with me at the locker, silently turned your back and either pretended not to notice or simply walked away, you need to understand this:

> **If you're not part of the solution then you are part of the problem.**

If you see someone being bullied and you do nothing, say nothing and pretend it didn't happen, your silence is empowering the bully. You are helping the bully tear down another person. You may not have uttered the hateful words or posted the mean comments, but if you see them or hear them and do nothing to stop them, you are allowing it to happen and thereby just as guilty.

You cannot feign innocence nor ignorance.

I've heard your many excuses:

"But if I say something to the bully then they might bully me, too." Maybe. But at least you won't be alone.

"If I speak up they might not be my friend anymore." Do you really want to be friends with someone who treats other people so badly?

> **Doing the right thing can be scary but it is your moral responsibility to PUT DOWN that fear and either stand up to the bully or report what you have witnessed.**

If you do nothing, you are helping the bully hurt people.

After I told the Principal what was happening to me, other kids who had experienced similar bullying from these girls or witnessed these girls bullying people came forward. For over two years I thought I was the only one being harassed. I thought I was alone... and all along, I wasn't alone. There were others like me and fear had silenced all of us. Our silence allowed the bullying to continue. Had the bystanders PUT DOWN that fear and spoken up sooner, so much pain could have been avoided.

> **When someone is being attacked, whether physically or emotionally, and you don't respond, your silence is viewed as an approval of the attack.**

Bystanders hold the most power in the fight against bullying. The victims are weakened and silenced by fear. The adults can't see the bullying because the bullies are too clever to behave badly in front of them. But you, bystanders, you see it happening and you hear it in the hallways, in the bathrooms, in the lunchrooms, on the playgrounds, in the classrooms, on the bus and via social media. You have the power to speak on behalf of the victim.

> ➢ **You never know when someone is hanging by their very last thread… when just one more mean word could end their life…or one nice word could literally save their life. Why wouldn't you choose to reach out and
utter the nice word?**

On the Bullied to Bold tour I have encountered many objections from bystanders, particularly when I challenge them toward action. I'd like to address several of the most common objections here.

OBJECTION 1: Bullying is such a huge problem that there is nothing I can do to change it. I'm just one person.

ANSWER: Change happens one person at a time. Every act of kindness matters. With your one nice word, you could save a life.

I want to share with you a story that someone posted on social media and when I read it, it gave me goosebumps. It drives home my whole point that one word or one action of kindness can literally save someone's life.

John was in sixth grade when he met Phil for the first time. John was walking home from school, carrying a bunch of school books. Three boys followed him, pushed him, made fun of him, knocked the books out of his hands and shoved him to the ground. Phil saw it happen from a distance and ran to help John. The mean boys had scattered by the time Phil arrived. He helped John pick up his books.

"Boy, you sure have a lot of books," Phil said. "Do you always take this many books home?"

John didn't answer, just sheepishly shrugged and resumed his walk toward home.

Being persistent, Phil pulled the top books from the pile. "Let me carry half," he said.

Over the course of the next several weeks, Phil walked John home every day, carrying half of his books. "You must be super smart if you study all these books every night," Phil remarked. It didn't take long for them to become friends and their friendship lasted all through middle school and all through high school.

At graduation, just before the ceremony, Phil found John backstage and wished him luck on his speech. See, John had become Valedictorian of their graduating class and it was his job to make the graduation speech.

Seeing that John was obviously nervous, Phil gave him a pat on the back and said, "Don't worry. You're gonna be great. You're the smartest guy I know…must have been from studying all those books every night." John smiled and then Phil took his seat in the auditorium and John took the stage.

Picking up the microphone, he paused for a moment and then began. "I want to tell you a story," he said. "It's about the day one person saved my life."

Phil's ears perked, as John had never shared this story with him before. Who had saved his life and how? Phil wondered.

"I was eleven years old and I was walking home from school. I was carrying a bunch of books because I had cleaned out my locker. I was going to go home and kill myself and I didn't want my mom to have to go back to the school and clean out my locker," John explained quietly, finding Phil in the crowd and making eye contact.

Tears filled Phil's eyes as he realized that that was the day he had met John.

"Then, one kid stopped to help me. He carried half of my books for me. He carried my books for the next several weeks and even though he never knew it, he carried me away from the idea of suicide. I'm here today because of the boy who had the courage to reach out to me when no one else would. That boy became my best friend and is still my best friend today. Thank you, Phil."

One person can make a difference. So, when you see someone sitting alone at the lunch table, go talk to them. Sometimes, just having a person next to you makes all the difference in the world.

OBJECTION 2: If I reach out to someone who is thought to be a "loser" then my reputation will be tarnished.

ANSWER: Is your reputation more important than someone's life? Because simply sitting next to someone who is not on your same social status just might give that person a reason to live one more day.

I don't care what label you've been given. If you're "popular", "a nerd", "a geek", "a weirdo", regardless of what you've been called, if you see someone who needs help, help them.

OBJECTION 3: I see bullying at school and on-line but I just feel that it is better not to get involved.

ANSWER: When you ignore an injustice you are validating the perpetrator. Your non-stance is a stance in and of itself, telling the victim that you believe they deserve to be attacked.

It is your moral obligation to either defend the victim or tell someone about the abuse you have witnessed.

OBJECTION 4: When I see cyberbullying, I attack back!

ANSWER: Though I understand the desire to attack back, more hate doesn't make things better. When you see mean, negative or hurtful comments, post something positive to counteract it. Kind words trump hate.

Cyberbullying is now considered a felony and will lead to expulsion from school and criminal charges. You don't want to get into trouble or be accused of cyberbullying because you were defending a friend, so keep your responses factual and positive.

OBJECTION 5: If I say anything to the bully then they won't be my friend anymore.

ANSWER: Why do you want to be friends with a bully in the first place? Are you doing the bully any good by protecting them? If there is a chance that you speaking up could open their eyes and change their behavior, isn't that a chance worth taking?

➢ **If one word or kind action from you could literally save someone's life, why wouldn't you make that choice?**

CHAPTER THIRTEEN

BULLIED TO BOLD

To all of you who have endured bullying, don't allow yourself to become bitter. It will only hurt you. Don't hold onto hate, it will only weigh you down. Let go of your anger and don't seek revenge.

> ➤ **Remember, success is the greatest revenge.**

Help those who are currently being bullied. Teach them to put down their fear, to break their silence, to build a support system and to stop the self-blame and shame.

If a bully apologizes to you, it's okay to forgive them. It doesn't mean you have to trust them or be friends with them, but sometimes forgiveness allows us to free ourselves of the pain they have caused and move on.

> ➢ **You don't forgive for their benefit, you do it for yours.**

My hope is that in sharing my experience you will know that you are not alone, that what you're feeling is normal, that there is a light at the end of the tunnel and that you have the strength to overcome.

Faith is important to me and an important part of who I am as a person, as a performer and as an artist. Everyone has their own level of faith and their own system of beliefs. It is often times in our darkest moments that we find out how deep our faith runs.

I believe in God and I know that even when we feel like we are at our loneliest and at our lowest, He is always with us. Through times of heartache and sadness, I cling to these two promises:

> ➢ **"I will never leave you nor forsake you."**
> Hebrews 13:5

> ➢ **"I can do all things through Christ who strengthens me."**
> Phillippians 4:13

So, put down your fear and transform from Bullied to Bold.

CHAPTER FOURTEEN

MY SONG

I wrote the song, PUT IT DOWN because I wanted to remind others to put down the things that hurt them and the things that they use to hurt themselves. It's human nature to cling to heartache, to replay mean words over and over in our minds and to focus on our fears and flaws. The song is a reminder to put those things down and rise above them.

I've written out the lyrics here so you can download the song from iTunes and sing along.

Breathe in and out. Scream out loud.
Just do what it takes to make it okay.

Put…Put it Down

You can't ignore the hurt inside. It just won't go away.

So many nights you lay and cry. Don't want to go another day.

Put it down. Put it down. Put it down. Put it down.

You don't need it anymore.

Put it down. Put it down. Put it down. Put it down.

And watch it as it hits the floor.

Now it's done, now it's through

Overcome, you're brand new

All that pain was yesterday.

Put it down. Put it down. Put it down. Down. Put it down.

You try every day to hold on but you break.

Your tears have all dried, but you're aching inside.

No one sees the pain.

You can't ignore the hurt inside. It just won't go away.

So many nights you lay and cry. Don't want to go another day.

Put it down. Put it down. Put it down. Put it down.
You don't need it anymore.
Put it down. Put it down. Put it down. Put it down.
And watch it as it hits the floor.
Now it's done, now it's through
Overcome, you're brand new
All that pain was yesterday.
Put it down. Put it down. Put it down. Down.
Put down that razor, you don't need no blade.
Put don't them pills, don't be ashamed.
Don't let the hurt keep you enslaved.
Put it down. Put it down. Put it down. Put it down.
You don't need it anymore.
Put it down. Put it down. Put it down. Put it down.
And watch it as it hits the floor.
Now it's done, now it's through
Overcome, you're brand new
All that pain was yesterday.
Put it down. Put it down. Put it down. Down.

So, put down your fear because together

we can

Stop the Hate Before it's Too Late.

The Bullied to Bold tour is run by
WTManagement and Global Publishing Group.
To book Maya Claridge into your classroom,
school assembly or youth organization, visit
www.BulliedToBold.com

Maya Claridge is a professional actress and singer with film, television, studio, stage and commercial experience. When she is not on location, on set, in studio or on stage, Maya is promoting her new hit single entitled, PUT IT DOWN. Using her talents and experience, Maya tours with Bullied to Bold, spreading a message of kindness and encouraging students to overcome bullying.

You may connect with Maya Claridge via the following social media channels:

        INSTAGRAM @maya.claridge

        SNAPCHAT maya.claridge

        FACEBOOK Maya Claridge

        TWITTER maya_claridge

        IMDB Maya Faith Claridge

Download PUT IT DOWN on iTunes today!

All pictures used in this book are courtesy of
WTManagement
© 2016 Global Publishing Group LLC